INTERNSHIP & VOLUNTEER OPPORTUNITIES

for People Who Love Animals

Ann Byers

ROSEN
PUBLISHING®
New York

Published in 2013 by The Rosen Publishing Group, Inc.
29 East 21st Street, New York, NY 10010

Copyright © 2013 by The Rosen Publishing Group, Inc.

First Edition

Library of Congress Cataloging-in-Publication Data

Byers, Ann.
Internship & volunteer opportunities for people who love animals/Ann Byers.
—1st ed.
    p. cm.—(A foot in the door)
Includes bibliographical references and index.
ISBN 978-1-4488-8293-9 (library binding)
1. Animal health—Juvenile literature. 2. Animal welfare—Vocational guidance—Juvenile literature. 3. Veterinary medicine—Vocational guidance—Juvenile literature. 4. Child volunteers. I. Title. II. Title: Internship and volunteer opportunities for people who love animals.
SF756.B94 2013
636.0890023—dc23
                                                        2012014789

Manufactured in the United States of America

CPSIA Compliance Information: Batch #W13YA: For further information, contact Rosen Publishing, New York, New York, at 1-800-237-9932.

Contents

This puppy's vest identifies him as an animal in training to become a guide dog for a visually impaired person. The head collar lets his trainer lead him gently, without pressure on his throat.

Introduction

Zeke already knew what taking care of a dog was like; he was largely responsible for the family pet. But when he agreed to take Danvers, caring for a dog became a completely different experience. It wasn't just that the black lab was considerably bigger than his dog. And it wasn't that, unlike his little dog, Danvers was a puppy. It was that someone was counting on him. This was more like a job, and how well he did it really mattered.

Zeke had joined a club, a group of volunteers who raise puppies for Guide Dogs for the Blind. Club members get the puppies used to being around people and animals, around noises and commotion. They train the puppies to obey simple commands. They get them ready for formal training to become guide dogs.

Danvers was fun for Zeke, but he had to follow very strict rules with him. He had to feed him specific food at certain times and in a certain manner. He had to teach him to sit, stay, come, and wait in exactly the ways club leaders told him. He had to work with him until Danvers mastered all the commands a person who is blind would give him.

Sometimes volunteering was challenging. Like the first few weeks, when the big dog, like most puppies, cried and barked at night. Or the time he drank from the toilet and got quite sick. But most of the time, having Danvers was great. Zeke learned techniques for handling and training a dog. With the club, he went to places he had never been before, and he made new friends. When Danvers completed the first phase of his training, Zeke was part of the graduation ceremony. And when he has finished all his schooling, Zeke will get to hand him off to the blind person he will help.

Zeke is too young to have a job, but he loves animals, and he is not too young to begin pursuing what he loves. Volunteering allows teens and adults to explore what they think they like…and discover what it's actually all about and if they really like it. For older teens, internships offer opportunities to learn even more. Different volunteer and internship experiences give people a taste of the many facets of working with animals.

There are many kinds of volunteer and internship experiences that involve animals. Whether you like cats or canaries, pugs or pigs, horses or seahorses, you can look for a place where you can be around those animals. And you can find opportunities to help, learn, or venture onto an exciting career path.

Chapter One

VOLUNTEERING AND INTERNING:
WIN-WIN PROPOSITIONS

Volunteering and interning can be gateways to jobs and careers. They are like doors that swing two ways: they are good for the job seeker and good for the employer. These experiences give the person looking for a job or career path a firsthand taste of what it might really be like to work at a particular type of job. At the same time, the person doing the hiring gets an idea of what kind of worker the volunteer or intern is likely to be.

Almost anyone can be a volunteer. A volunteer is simply someone who works without pay. Some volunteers work regularly, several hours a day or a few hours per week or month. Others work occasionally, usually on projects.

Volunteering

People volunteer for a number of different reasons. Often they support the work of an organization and want to help the cause. Some people volunteer because they know the experience will help them grow personally. It may help

Volunteers and staff members of the Lowry Park Manatee Rehabilitation Center in Florida release a manatee back into the wild. The injured manatee was rescued and nursed back to health at the center.

them overcome shyness, gain self-confidence, and become more responsible.

Some volunteer because doing so gives them a chance to do something they could not do otherwise. How many teens can afford to spend a summer in a national park? How many have opportunities to groom horses, feed sharks, or rehabilitate birds? These are some of the interesting jobs volunteers can do.

Some people volunteer because they want to do something worthwhile with their time and talents. It is a very good feeling to know you are helping an animal or another person. Even people who volunteer only because the experience sounds fun or because it is an assignment frequently discover that they are making a difference in someone's life or in the community. And that is very rewarding.

Community Service and Service Learning

Some schools have recognized the value to students and communities of having students volunteer. Many have begun to incorporate service projects into their curriculum, requiring students to participate in a specified number of service hours. Some schools give students credit toward graduation for their participation in community service. Community service projects are short-term activities that benefit the community. Sometimes students have to find their own projects and sometimes schools, clubs, churches, and other organizations take on a group project. The Animal Humane Society has a list of ideas for service projects that help animals (http://www.animalhumanesociety.org/webfm_send/254).

Many schools are going beyond community service and inviting students to become involved in service learning. Service learning is community service with an educational component attached. It is much more involved than simply volunteering. Students perform a service that meets a community need, and a teacher helps the students use that service as a learning activity. Service learning requires preparation, reflection, action, and demonstration. For example, a service-learning project to raise money to add more space to an animal shelter might look like the following:

In preparation, students learn about the shelter: what it does in the community, how it operates, and how it gets and spends money. The students visit the shelter and talk with people who work there. They see the conditions of the shelter and understand why more space is needed. They might interview people in the community to find out how they feel about the work the shelter is doing. They might calculate how many additional animals could be saved and adopted if the funds were raised and the new facility built.

The teacher leads the students as they reflect on their findings, asking what they learned, what they think, and how to proceed. Reflection continues throughout the action phase, as the students decide how to raise money and then carry out their plan. When the project is completed, the service learning is not over. Students must demonstrate what they learned. They may make presentations to other students at the school or to community groups. They may create and print flyers the shelter can distribute, write letters to the editor, or design a Web page showing the need and the progress toward meeting the need.

Service learning is a win for everyone. The school benefits because the project

This volunteer from California helped care for animals in a shelter in Joplin, Missouri, where hundreds of dogs and cats rescued after the 2011 tornado awaited their owners.

furthers its educational goals—students apply what they have been learning to real-life situations. The organization hosting the volunteers wins because it receives help, it exposes young people to its cause, and it engages them in a way that may keep them committed for a lifetime. The community is better because the project enables the organization to do more good work. And the students are the big winners. They learn information and gain skills, they receive school credit, they have a great experience they can add to their résumé, and they make contacts they can use later.

Internship

Community and service learning are short-term, unpaid experiences. They usually involve a project rather than an ongoing commitment. An internship, on the other hand, lasts longer and interns may receive some pay—but not always. An internship is a job that is also a learning opportunity. It is a kind of on-the-job training for people who are interested in a particular field of work but have little or no experience in the field. Interns can try out a career path and see if they like it before they invest a lot of time and money into meeting the requirements for the career.

For example, becoming a veterinarian requires a bachelor's degree, which takes at least four years to earn—and four more years of education after that. What if after eight years of schooling a student finds that he or she does not enjoy the job? It would be far better to discover that early in the process! It is also possible that during the internship that same veterinary student realizes that he or she loves birds, is really good with small mammals, or is fascinated with the research aspect of the job.

Unusual White House Pets

Nearly all of the U.S. presidents had pets with them when they lived in the White House. There were more dogs at the White House than any other animal. The second most popular pet? A horse. George Washington, who lived in Mount Vernon because the White House wasn't built yet, had twelve horses, as well as thirty-six dogs and a parrot. In addition to the common pets—cats, rabbits, guinea pigs, hamsters, and birds—some more unusual animals have lived at the White House, including the following:

- Lions, tigers, and bears
- Sheep, cows, goats, and pigs
- Bobcats, wildcats, and coyotes
- A donkey, zebra, and hyena
- Snakes, lizards, and an alligator
- A wallaby, pygmy hippo, and herd of elephants

Only three presidents had no pets, including Millard Fillmore, who was a founder and president of a chapter of the American Society for the Prevention of Cruelty to Animals.

An internship can help steer the intern toward a specific career goal within a larger field.

Some companies pay interns a small salary, and some give them a stipend that covers some of their expenses. But internships

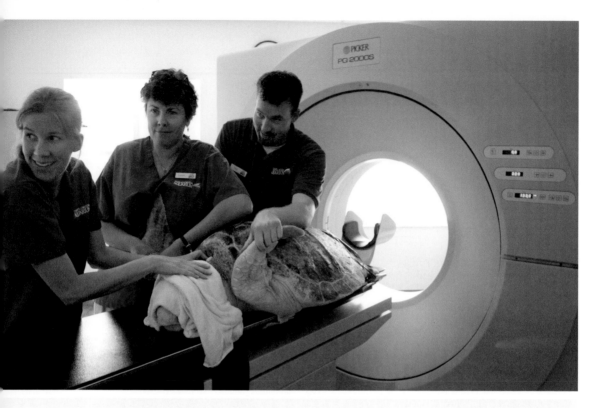

An intern *(left)* in an aquarium assists a veterinary technician preparing a turtle for a CT scan. The turtle was undergoing treatment after being injured by a propeller.

in animal science, zoology, veterinary science, and similar fields are often with nonprofit organizations. Most nonprofits do not pay interns, but the unpaid interns greatly benefit from their experience. They receive school credit, which brings them closer to graduation and their career goals. They gain invaluable training that builds their skills and enhances any job application. And because they often work under mentors, they form professional and sometimes personal relationships with people who may have connections and influence in the field in which the interns want to work. Like volunteer and service learning experiences, internships are win-win opportunities.

Chapter Two

HOW TO START

F inding a place to volunteer with animals is not difficult. Finding a position doing exactly what you want may take a little more work. Just as there are entry-level jobs that can be performed with no skills and higher-level jobs that require some experience, there are different levels of volunteer positions. And there are a number of ways to find them.

Local Organizations and Businesses

If you are looking for an entry-level volunteer opportunity, one of the easiest ways to start is to visit organizations in your community that care for animals. Animal shelters, rescue groups, and clinics need people to help with simple tasks, so they have volunteer jobs that anyone can do. They are usually nonprofits, so they often welcome extra pairs of hands. Most shelters have a volunteer department

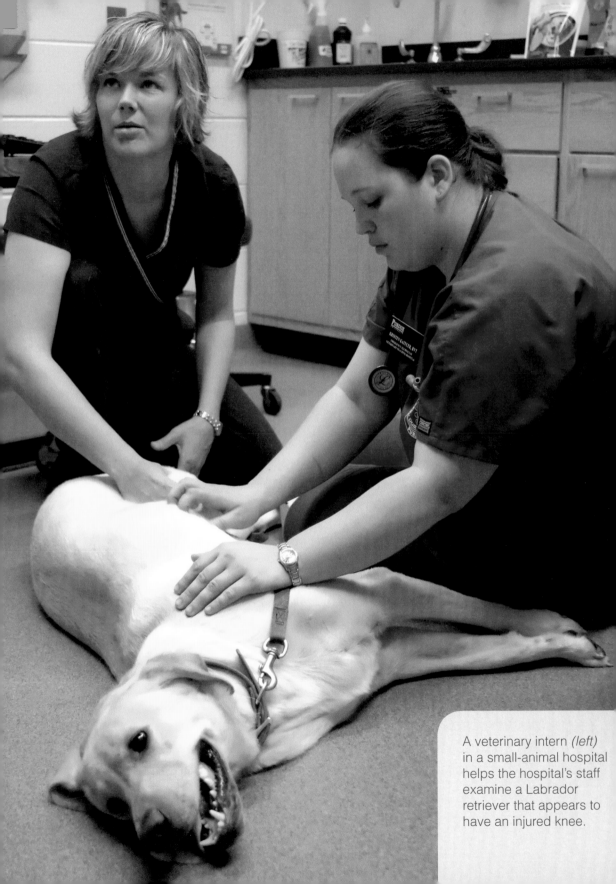

A veterinary intern *(left)* in a small-animal hospital helps the hospital's staff examine a Labrador retriever that appears to have an injured knee.

or volunteer coordinator. To begin volunteering, you simply need to call or visit the local organization.

Nonprofit agencies are not the only organizations that use volunteers. Some businesses also have room for unpaid help. If you want to work with animals, look for all the places in your community where animals might be: pet stores, kennels, groomers, and pet sitters. Look in a print or online telephone directory under the headings "Animal" and "Pet." You might consider not limiting yourself to working with dogs and cats. Check also under the headings "Bird," "Horse," "Stable," "Fish," and "Reptile." If you live in a rural area, don't neglect farms and ranches. Farm animals require work, and some farmers and ranchers may be happy to accept volunteer help.

One of the best ways to get a foot in the door of a local business is to have someone else open it for you. Talk with people you know who have pets. Find out what services they use and ask if they will give you a referral. At the very least, mentioning your connection to a satisfied customer will impress managers when you ask if you can volunteer at their business.

Online

A number of organizations, especially larger ones, post volunteer opportunities on their Web sites. Typing "Volunteer with animals" into a search engine yields hundreds of possibilities. Some are volunteer matching sites that enable users to search for openings by geographic location and interest. Others are agencies that offer volunteer positions. The Web sites of national animal welfare organizations have links to the sites of their local chapters, and the local chapter sites have information about volunteering.

Some organizations to look up are: the Humane Society of the United States, the American Society for the Prevention of Cruelty to Animals, and the Audubon Society.

The Internet is a great help for people who want to work with specific animals or in a particular type of animal care. Entering "Volunteer birds," "Volunteer snakes," "Volunteer animal sanctuary," "Volunteer animal rescue," or "Volunteer animal assisted therapy," for example, brings up a number of opportunities. Since there are fewer of these kinds of positions than jobs in shelters, volunteers may have to travel to take advantage of them.

People willing to travel can find summer or other short-term, intensive volunteer or intern positions online. Camps, zoos, nature centers, and wildlife preserves recruit volunteers. Some of these short-term programs include housing, food, and other costs, and volunteers may be required to pay something to participate. Other programs may give volunteers a small stipend. Many short-term placements entail travel expenses.

Zoos give volunteers who live far from the ocean experience with marine animals. Here, German race car driver Heinz-Harald Frentzen feeds dolphins at the Indianapolis City Zoo.

For those who can afford the cost, the Internet lists a number of organizations that offer volunteer and intern experiences in other countries. People with no skills can help raise lion cubs in South Africa, protect sea turtles in Costa Rica, or feed rescued monkeys in Ecuador. These kinds of opportunities can be for as brief as a week or as long as a year.

School Placement

Everyone does not have the time or money for intensive, short-term programs. But everyone can volunteer. If students cannot find suitable places to volunteer on their own, they can get help from guidance counselors or the career placement office at their school. The counselor's job is to help students progress toward their career goals, and volunteering is one step in that process. Counselors frequently have lists of organizations looking for volunteers, and they match students with agencies that need help.

School counselors can also set up group projects for students who want to perform community service or be involved in service learning. Other sources for these projects are youth groups and clubs such as Scouts and 4-H. Many communities have youth service clubs specifically designed to help young people find places to volunteer.

Just as high schools can help teens discover volunteer opportunities, colleges can help their students find internships. Schools that offer programs in animal science, zoology, or veterinary medicine generally have lists of organizations—typically nonprofits—that welcome college interns. The majority of internships with nonprofit organizations are unpaid. In fact, students

A sixteen-year-old girl cares for her horse at a 4-H horse camp. At horse camps, 4-H members learn and improve riding and showmanship skills.

may need to pay the organization for the privilege of interning. This fee covers the organization's expenses in providing instructors and mentors and doing the paperwork required for the intern to receive college credit.

Volunteering: Steps to a Career

From fragile butterflies to lumbering rhinos, seventeen-year-old Taylor Baker has seen them all...up close and personal. His love of animals and his willingness to give of his time have opened up adventures that he calls "amazing." These adventures began when he was in junior high. Taylor volunteered to talk with visitors to the Butterfly Gardens, explaining the interactions between plants and insects. In ninth grade, he enrolled in his school's junior zoo crew service-learning program. Serving as a zoo interpreter, he described the habits and habitats of farm animals, animals native to his state, and exotic animals to visitors at the Maryland Zoo. The volunteer experiences convinced him that he wanted to pursue a career in zoo science. He took a four-week summer course so he could become a junior zookeeper. Now Taylor spends much of his spare time at the African Watering Hole with zebras, giraffes, rhinos, and ostriches. He not only feeds and cares for them, but he also creates and conducts enrichment activities for them. Taylor has received two national President's Volunteer Service Awards for more than 670 hours of volunteer service to the zoo. More important than the awards to Taylor is the fact that his volunteer experience will help him reach his childhood dream—working in a zoo.

The Process

Although many organizations need and welcome volunteers and interns, they do not necessarily accept everyone who applies. Many, but not all, have a lower age limit of sixteen, eighteen, or twenty. Some require certain skills or experience. Organizations and businesses often treat volunteers and interns like unpaid employees, so securing a volunteer or intern position is much like getting a job. It may entail an application, an interview, perhaps an essay, and sometimes an application fee.

Employers expect volunteers and interns to treat the position with the same level of seriousness they do. They expect them to keep to their schedule, arrive on time, work hard, and have a good attitude. If volunteers live up to these very basic expectations, they will have a referral that will look good on any résumé, whether they decide to pursue a career that involves animals or not. On top of that, they will have a rewarding experience. Whether they volunteer as a stepping-stone to a job or simply for fun, their service makes a difference for an animal, and that makes volunteering a serious business.

Chapter Three

IN THE WILD

People wanting to volunteer with animals need to go where the animals are. It is easy to find dogs, cats, and other typical pets. But there are also opportunities for working with exotic (non-native) creatures, wild animals, birds, sea animals, and other less common creatures. These opportunities are found in zoos, aquariums, nature centers, and wildlife sanctuaries and preserves.

Zoos and Aquariums

There are 225 zoos and aquariums in the United States accredited with the Association of Zoos and Aquariums. The Canadian Association of Zoos and Aquariums accredits twenty-five. Most of these offer a variety of volunteer and internship opportunities. Some accept volunteers as young as fourteen—even younger if they volunteer alongside one of their parents. Many require volunteers to be at least eighteen. Zoos and aquariums need volunteers year-round, and they have teen volunteer or junior zookeeper programs in the summer. Summer programs require a little more from the volunteer; usually they include classroom instruction. With the additional education, the volunteer gains new skills and has the ability to do more.

Some of the entry-level tasks put volunteers in close contact with the animals. They might prepare different types of food: cut up watermelons for bears, chop fruits and vegetables for birds, or

When more sea lions than usual along the California coast appeared to be sick or weak, the Marine Mammal Center just north of San Francisco enlisted the help of volunteers. Above, a volunteer feeds herring to undernourished sea lions at the rescue and education center.

make fish milkshakes for dolphins. They can provide enrichment activities for the animals. Animals in captivity can become bored, lazy, or frustrated without the challenges and wide-open spaces of their natural habitats. Zookeepers devise puzzles, toys, and games that enrich the animals' environment. These objects and activities simulate some of the animals' native environment, helping them exercise and retain their natural skills. Volunteers might find clever ways to hide a deer's food so that it has to hunt for it, make puzzle feeders from coconuts to keep monkeys curious, or fill new mud wallows for rhinos or warthogs. And cages and pens always need to be cleaned. None of these jobs require special skills, but in doing them, volunteers gain knowledge and skills.

Direct animal care is not the only possibility for working in zoos and aquariums. Teens, as well as adults, can become education volunteers, or docents. Docents must attend classes to learn about the animals and their habitats. They talk to visitors and answer their questions. Volunteer educators help them enjoy and learn from their visit. They are the ones who show children how to pick up starfish, brush and pet goats, and find camouflaged lizards.

Volunteers are also needed to keep zoos and aquariums in top shape and running smoothly. Conservation volunteers build and repair animal enclosures and help restore habitats. Research volunteers observe animals and record their behaviors. Visitor service volunteers man the gates, ticket booths, and gift shops.

Sanctuaries and Nature Centers

The purpose of zoos is to house animals so that people can see them. Sanctuaries, also called animal preserves, house animals so they can survive. They are homes for abandoned, abused,

Teens Can Make a Difference

Two aging bears had an impact on young Justin Barker. Barker was thirteen years old when he first saw the twins Brutus and Ursula. They were huddled together in a small cage in a city park in Roseville, California, not far from Sacramento. They had spent all eighteen years of their lives in the cramped enclosure. The little park had once housed a small zoo, but because of repeated flooding, the other animals had been gradually removed. Only the two black bears remained.

Their conditions saddened Justin. Their cage was so small that Brutus had worn a path in the concrete as he paced back and forth. Sometimes the bears slipped on the algae that covered the cement. Without trees or other shade, the only relief from the California heat was a pool of dirty water. The park staff fed the bears, but they were not trained in caring for the animals.

Justin decided to do something about the situation. Twenty miles (32.2 kilometers) away, in the city of Folsom, was a well-tended animal sanctuary and zoo. Couldn't Brutus and Ursula be moved there? He called the town's mayor and was told it would take at least $60,000 to relocate the twins. Undaunted, Justin launched a campaign to raise the money. At age fourteen, Justin Barker became an animal activist.

It took almost three years of phone calls, letters, and speeches, but by 1999 the Roseville Bear Relocation Project had raised $250,000 and the two bears were happy in their new home.

and injured animals. The animals live in protected conditions as close to their natural habitat as possible. Some injured animals are rehabilitated and returned to the wild, but most live the rest of their lives in the preserves. Aquariums often serve as sanctuaries,

American Ashley Robertson won a contest that allows her to volunteer with giant pandas in China. Every day she cleans one panda's cage, prepares its meals of bamboo, plays with it, and records its activities.

places where hurt or orphaned sea mammals are rescued and cared for until they can return to the ocean.

Volunteers and interns in wildlife preserves perform the same kinds of tasks as zoo volunteers: animal care, education, conservation, research, and visitor services. They may have more opportunities for hands-on experience with the animals, as animals in sanctuaries require more care. Volunteers might assist vets treating injured animals, hand-feed babies, band birds, or trim horses' hooves. They might teach an orphaned bear cub to forage for food and see it return to its natural habitat.

Sanctuaries provide environments that are close to animals' natural conditions, but nature centers *are* the animals' original habitats. Nature centers are areas kept in their natural state. They are large tracts of land without houses or other human developments that preserve the plants and animals native to the area. Nature centers allow people to experience specific natural environments—deserts, marshes, canyons, forests, bayous, areas surrounding rivers, etc. Like sanctuaries, nature centers rely on volunteers and interns. Volunteers and interns serve as educators, help feed and care for the wildlife, collect information for research, and make visitors welcome.

Working with animals in the wild, especially in summer or other intensive programs, often demands physical strength. Volunteers may have to traipse through fields, lift heavy bags, pitch hay, construct buildings, or mend fences. They may work long hours in a desert climate or at a high altitude. They will be dirty and tired. But if they love animals, they will probably love every minute of it.

Chapter Four

ANIMAL "HOMES" AND "HOTELS"

B y far, the greatest volunteer option for people who love animals is the local animal shelter. Shelters are temporary homes for animals awaiting permanent placement. The American Society for the Prevention of Cruelty to Animals estimates there are five thousand independent animal shelters in the United States. They receive from five to seven million animals every year. That is an average of at least five thousand dogs and cats per shelter.

In addition to shelters, volunteer opportunities await in boarding kennels. Kennels are more like animal "hotels." They are places that care for animals when the pets' owners are not at home for a period of time. Generally, kennels provide accommodations for dogs; hotels for cats are called catteries. Some facilities accept both dogs and cats. Large boarding kennels usually house animals in cages or other structures—called kennels—but some small ones take care of the pets in private homes.

Opportunities are also available at doggie daycares. Unlike kennels, which keep pets overnight, daycares tend dogs during the day, usually for owners who work. They may have onetime canine "clients," but dogs are typically enrolled for daily or regular care. Like daycares for children, doggie daycares become very familiar "homes away from home" for many pets. In addition to their primary functions, shelters, kennels, and doggie daycares often offer services such as grooming and training.

Shelters operate with limited funds; most could not exist without volunteers. Although boarding kennels, catteries, and doggie daycares are profit-making businesses, many are also happy to have volunteers help provide the care and love their animals need.

During times of crisis, animal shelters can be overcrowded. This volunteer from New Orleans gives some much-needed exercise to a dog rescued after the Joplin, Missouri, tornado.

When a Kentucky canine shelter underwent renovations, project volunteers helped care for the dogs that were temporarily displaced. This volunteer is being thanked.

Entry-Level Tasks

Some of the necessary tasks at shelters, kennels, and daycares are very simple. Almost anyone can clean cages and kennels and feed and water animals. Some of the entry-level jobs involve direct contact with the facilities' animals. Because the dogs in shelters, kennels, and daycares have to be confined, they also have to be exercised. Volunteers with little experience can easily take dogs for walks (or runs!) or play with them in exercise yards. Cats also need room to play, and they love human stimulation. Just playing with animals is a valuable contribution volunteers make.

Some shelter animals have been mistreated. As a result, they are afraid of people. The goal of shelters is to find good homes for these animals, but few people want to adopt frightened animals. Neglected and abused animals need lots of holding, petting, and loving to heal and trust humans. Shelters also take in wild animals; they are also hard to adopt. Volunteers socialize these cats and dogs—get them used to being around people.

Owners and managers do not take volunteers for granted. They pay attention to how they discharge the duties assigned to them and how they interact with the animals and with people. Volunteers who perform simple tasks well and cheerfully are often invited to be trained for work that is a little more demanding or that requires specific knowledge or skills.

Some Experience or Training Required

Handling animals beyond petting and walking them often takes additional training. Volunteers may be taught to bathe dogs, brush

In his three-month internship in the avian department of Florida's Palm Beach Zoo, this high school student learned to feed baby parrots.

both cats and dogs, trim nails, and perform other basic grooming. In shelters, dogs may need to be trained to use a leash and respond to simple commands. Skilled volunteers can assist in this training.

Everything in a shelter is aimed at finding the animals permanent homes. Shelters need volunteers who can talk to people who want to adopt about the behaviors of different breeds and the animals that are available. Some people come to the shelter for their first pet, and they may have questions. Volunteers learn how to tell a dog's age, how to know how big an animal may become, and whether a particular pet is likely to be suitable for young children. Some shelters take their animals to pet stores and other places where people who want to adopt may come. They also hold special adopt-a-pet events. Volunteers are needed to transport the animals to and from these places, handle them in the unfamiliar settings, answer questions, and fill out paperwork. These jobs require not only skills in animal handling, but also broad knowledge and the ability to communicate well with people.

Shelters usually have an area for stray animals that have been picked up or brought to the facility. The animals are kept here for a certain period of time to give their owners a chance to find and claim them. Workers in this part of a shelter answer phone calls about lost or found pets, fill out reports, take animals in, check their condition, and guide hopeful owners looking for their pets. Volunteers can do any of these tasks.

There are also volunteer jobs at shelters, kennels, and daycares that do not have direct contact with the animals. Office helpers are always appreciated—people who enter data into computers, manage files, and make phone calls. Photographers are in demand; they take and post pictures of animals awaiting adoption, of satisfied kennel "clients," and of happy dogs at daycares. People who are willing to clean feeding dishes and equipment or wash and fold bedding, towels, and other laundry are invaluable.

Volunteers Always Have Work

Since she was a little girl, Mary Baker wanted to be a zoologist. Also since she was little, she has had a special affection for animals that are hurt, shy, or frightened. Her two dogs and horse were rescued animals. So as soon as she was old enough, at age twelve, Mary began volunteering at a nonprofit animal rescue organization. Every Saturday she takes dogs and cats that have been rescued to a pet food store, where people see them and, she hopes, decide to adopt them.

Volunteering once a week is not enough for Mary. She also helps out at a local animal shelter and at the Humane Society. Mary, who is now sixteen years old, cleans cages and walks dogs. She believes so strongly in the work of these animal welfare agencies that she spends her after-school time keeping the rescue organization's Web site up to date. And she takes part in its fund-raisers.

Mary volunteers because she loves animals, not because volunteering can be a step to a career. Still, when she applies for a job as a zoologist someday, her many hours with rescued and sheltered animals are sure to be noticed.

Homes for Horses

Some people who love animals are particularly fond of horses. Volunteer and internship opportunities with horses are available at stables, ranches, and camps. Some of these places give riding and horsemanship lessons, some practice equine-assisted therapy, and some do both. Some ranches are sanctuaries for rescued horses. Entry-level volunteers clean stalls, take care of equipment, bathe and groom the horses, and exercise them. Sometimes volunteers also help maintain the facility; they repair buildings, paint fences, and tend to the grounds. Those with experience may work as wranglers—horse handlers. Wranglers guide horses to and from their stalls and may lead them or walk alongside riders.

People with some experience who are enrolled in certain college programs can take advantage of a number of internship

Volunteers help children in a California equine therapy program. This boy is strengthening his leg muscles by learning to post—to lift himself out of the saddle slightly at the right times as the horse walks.

opportunities on ranches. Interns are usually exploring or pursuing careers in equine management, farm or ranch management, horse breeding, equine veterinary services, horse training, equine-assisted therapy, or horse rescue and rehabilitation. Some internships are residential, requiring students to live and work on the ranch for several weeks or months, often for much of a school semester. Nonresidential internships are also available.

Challenges

Volunteering in animal homes and hotels can be challenging. The environment is noisy and smelly. The work is somewhat demanding physically. Some of the jobs require being outdoors no matter what the weather is like. Although the facilities take every safety precaution, animals do scratch and bite. Perhaps the greatest challenges are emotional. Volunteers can become attached to certain animals and those animals eventually leave the facility. Volunteers may have difficulty seeing animals that have been mistreated or knowing that some are euthanized. But usually the rewards of helping an animal recover from abuse, get the exercise and care it needs, or go to a loving home outweigh the challenges.

Chapter Five

PLACES THAT SERVE ANIMALS

W hether they live in a zoo, a nature center, a shelter, or a home with a family, animals benefit from services that humans can provide. Veterinarians, groomers, and people who supply food and equipment for animals keep them healthy and happy. Volunteers are not as critical to these service providers as they are in some of the nonprofits described earlier. But these areas offer wonderful volunteer opportunities.

They do not, however, offer internships. In veterinary practice, as in human medicine, the term "intern" is reserved for a person who has graduated from veterinary or medical school and earned the title and degree of doctor. A veterinarian who pursues clinical, or practical, training is an intern. The other service areas—grooming and pet supply—don't require licenses or extensive training; therefore, they don't offer internships.

Animal Hospitals and Clinics

Hospitals keep animals overnight; clinics perform procedures and send the patient home. Animal hospitals are usually clinics, too, and there are many clinics that are not hospitals. In addition to traditional veterinary offices, there are mobile shot clinics that

Animal hospitals, clinics, and grooming businesses sometimes need volunteers to answer phones, make appointments, and greet pet owners. Volunteers get to work near animals, and they also gain office skills.

move from place to place dispensing vaccinations. Shelters have clinics where vets examine new arrivals before they are placed with other animals, give the necessary shots, spay and neuter pets before they are adopted, and give whatever medical treatment the shelter animals need. Clinics and veterinarians often specialize, working primarily with one or perhaps two types of "client." The most common specialties are horses, food animals (cows, pigs, sheep), exotic animals, large animals, small animals, marine mammals, and birds. Some work exclusively with companion animals (pets).

In animal clinics, volunteers can do a number of front-office tasks, where they interact with both people and their pets. They can check animals in and out and explain the treatment or services the clinic will provide. Knowledgeable volunteers can also answer questions about general pet care. They can help with answering phones, making appointments, billing, and other paperwork. When owners come to claim their pets after surgery, volunteers may bring the animals to them and help them understand post-operation instructions.

In the back office—the clinical area—volunteers can begin with entry-level assignments and build up their knowledge and skills. Wherever there are animals, there is always a need for mopping, doing laundry, cleaning, and disinfecting. Instruments and materials used for surgeries must be sterilized. Supplies need to be unpacked and put away. Vets may want help weighing animals and placing and holding them on exam tables. Animals recovering from surgery need to be watched carefully. As volunteers perform these tasks well, they may be asked to assist with some of the medical procedures.

From Animal Shelter to Hollywood Star

Frank Inn had a soft spot for shelter dogs; he felt a little like one of them. As a young man, he had nearly been killed in a car accident, and someone rescued him. So when he wanted a dog, he went to an animal shelter. That's where he found Higgins.

Inn trained animals that performed in movies and on television. He trained some animals that were very famous: Asta, Lassie, and a pig named Arnold. Inn's animals won more than forty PATSY (Performing Animal Top Star of the Year) Awards. Higgins was just a puppy when Inn adopted him, but before long he was a star. Inn changed his name to Benji, and the dog appeared in numerous television programs and starred in three movies.

Benji was so popular that his movies sparked the adoption of more than one million dogs from shelters. People were particularly interested in mutts—mixed-breed dogs like Benji. Benji was not only a successful actor, but he was also a very busy activist. He and Inn made many appearances to promote adoption from animal shelters and other animal and humanitarian causes.

Pet Groomers

Veterinarians are concerned with animals' health; groomers take care of their appearance. They usually work with dogs, but a few also see cats. Groomers may work in a shelter, kennel, veterinary clinic, or pet store. Many have their own businesses, usually a salon where owners bring their pets. Some operate mobile businesses, going to the pet owners' homes.

With each animal, groomers begin with a rough cut of the coat. Then they give a bath, taking care to select the shampoo

This groomer must thin the Pomeranian's soft, thick undercoat before she can cut its coarser outer coat or its fluffy tail. Groomers must learn the correct cut for each breed.

that is best for the dog. After the bath and blow-dry, the animal has its nails trimmed and its ears and feet cleaned. Some groomers also clean the teeth. Then comes the final cut: the groomer trims, brushes, combs, and shapes the dog's coat according to the particular breed.

Groomers are not merely dog barbers and beauticians. They help keep animals healthy, which is one reason shelters often have groomers. Bathing dogs, conditioning their fur, and getting rid of fleas are important to their well-being. In addition, groomers get underneath the coat to the skin, and that enables them to spot sores, wounds, or other conditions that might be health concerns.

Grooming is not an easy job. The dogs and cats that groomers see are often nervous, frightened, or aggressive, so they may try to bite or scratch. Some come in with badly matted fur, and some have fleas. It takes a great deal of skill to style an animal's coat, and it is not something with which a groomer can use help. About the only volunteer opportunity in pet grooming is bathing dogs. It may seem like a small opportunity, but it can be the start of a career path. No state requires groomers to be licensed, so people frequently enter the field by being apprentices—working with and learning from a professional groomer. Many began their apprenticeships as volunteer bathers.

Chapter Six

CLUBS AND THERAPY PROGRAMS

One form of volunteering is joining clubs. Participating in clubs does not give people the emotional reward of helping a cause, but it does enable them to gain knowledge and skills that will be helpful for anyone interested in a career that involves animals. Clubs generally require that members have their own animals. The most common types of clubs for animals and their owners are 4-H clubs, kennel clubs for dogs, and pony clubs for horses.

4-H Clubs

4-H clubs are youth development organizations. Club members work together on projects, and as they do, they develop personal qualities and social confidence in addition to specific skills. 4-H has broadened beyond its initial emphasis on agriculture and raising animals to include environmental science, technology, energy, and any other

4-H club members raise and show a variety of animals. This Michigan girl has a lionhead rabbit. In addition to providing typical care for rabbits, she has to brush her long-haired pet every week.

idea a club comes up with. Each club decides on its own projects. The philosophy of the clubs is that young people learn by doing.

In some clubs that choose animal projects, members raise animals that are used for meat: cows, pigs, or sheep. They learn how to care for the animal and how to show it—present it so that people can see its value. When it is full-grown, it is auctioned off and sold. In other clubs, members raise cows and goats that will be used for milking or horses, rabbits, chickens, dogs, or cats. They show the animals that are not destined for meat production, but they do not sell them.

As part of the learn-by-doing approach, 4-H clubs have curricula that members study. The veterinary science curriculum teaches basic animal anatomy, explains normal and abnormal conditions in animals, and gives an overview of the careers that are available in the veterinary field. Lessons on horses include equine care, horse behavior, and riding and showing the animal. Members with dog projects study dog health and care, breeding, and training. They also learn about service dogs.

Membership in 4-H is open to those ages nine through nineteen, and most states have junior programs for children ages five through nine and programs for college-age youths. People can become involved by joining a club, going to a 4-H camp, or participating in a project sponsored by a club. Many 4-H clubs conduct community service projects.

Kennel Clubs

For people who are interested primarily in dogs, kennel clubs are good tools for learning, acquiring skills, and meeting people in the pet industry. A kennel club is an association for owners of purebred dogs. Its purpose is to promote breeding, studying, training, and showing purebred dogs. There are clubs exclusively for one breed, such as boxer, bulldog, or poodle clubs, and there are clubs that accept several breeds. The American Kennel Club (AKC), the most well-known kennel club in the United States, keeps a registry (list) of purebred dogs of many breeds, detailing each dog's parents and date of birth. It also puts on dog shows at

Young people compete in the Junior Showmanship event at the Westminster Kennel Club Dog Show in New York City. The annual show has been held since 1877.

which dogs of the same breed compete in looks and performing the functions considered standard for the breed.

The AKC and other clubs have opportunities for juniors, ages nine to eighteen. These include classes in dog handling. Juniors learn basic techniques for handling any dog, as well as methods specific to their breeds. They learn how to show their pets. They can participate in Junior Showmanship competitions where they, not their dogs, are judged. Junior competitions are held in conjunction with the regular dog shows, and this gives teens a chance to interact with owners, handlers, trainers, judges, and groomers.

Internship Helps Sea Creatures

Sean Russell couldn't get the pictures out of his head. Dolphins thrashing about, trying to disentangle themselves from nylon cord. Gulls dangling from the strands hung up in tree branches. Sea creatures were dying because of carelessly discarded fishing line. The images were part of a marine biologist's presentation Sean had seen in high school. When he entered college as a biology major, he decided to study the situation.

As a college student, Sean was able to secure an internship with a biologist. One of his projects was to find a safe, inexpensive way for fishermen to dispose of their used lines. The biologist who was mentoring him had an idea: have the fishermen put their old lines in tennis ball cans, collect the cans, and recycle the lines. The idea was great, but Sean couldn't carry it out by himself. He would need teams of volunteers. He presented the plan to his 4-H club, and the Stow-It—Don't Throw It project was born.

The project not only helps sea creatures, but it also empowers youth to care about the marine environment and be part of the solution to a very serious problem. Individuals and groups collect recycled tennis ball cans; transform them into temporary recycling bins for discarded fishing line; and distribute them to fishermen at piers, tackle shops, and other places. The project has expanded to encompass hundreds of young volunteers in seventeen counties in Florida, and it has saved countless dolphins and birds. It began with one person in a college internship.

Pony Clubs

For youth who love horses, pony clubs offer fun, education, and skill development. Pony clubs are usually operated for children and teens by parents and other adult volunteers. As with 4-H and kennel clubs, pony club members must have their own animal, either a horse or a pony. A few clubs meet at centers where horses are available for club members to lease if they do not have their own.

Pony clubs have mounted meetings and unmounted meetings. At the mounted meetings, members hone their riding skills by riding, jumping, and participating in sports on horseback. At the unmounted meetings, they learn about horse management: what to feed their horses and how much feed costs, when and why to visit the vet, and how much the horse can carry and pull. They learn about horseshoes, breeding, grooming, and first aid. They are taught how to choose, use, and care for tack (saddles and other equipment). As they become good at using the information they learn, the older members become instructors for the younger ones. Teaching builds their confidence and skills even more, making pony clubs great places for anyone who wants to pursue a career with horses.

Pony club members learn that horses have small stomachs so they need to be fed small amounts of grass or hay several times each day. They like an occasional apple or carrot.

Animal-Assisted Therapy

One career path for people who love horses—or dogs, cats, birds, or other small animals—is animal-assisted therapy. Anyone who loves animals knows that being with an animal can lift people's spirits. That is what animal-assisted therapy is all about: putting a carefully screened animal next to a person who needs a boost of some kind—some motivation or a reason to smile. Pet owners regularly take their pets to hospitals, nursing homes, youth detention facilities, children's shelters, and other places where people

In many homes for senior citizens, regular visits from therapy animals brighten residents' days. This dog's jacket identifies the animal as approved for such visits: trained, gentle, and friendly.

are confined. The animals cheer the people up. In one program, volunteers take their dogs to libraries, where children who are otherwise reluctant to open books read to them. Technically, the connection between human and animal is not therapy unless a licensed therapist includes it in a patient's treatment plan; it is actually an animal-assisted activity (AAA).

An AAA is a volunteer opportunity for someone who owns a friendly pet. Almost any small animal can be a good therapy animal, even a guinea pig or a rat. The animal needs to be gentle and calm, and the owner needs to be trained in handling the animal during the visit. Some large hospitals, nursing homes, and humane societies provide training for people who want to volunteer in AAA, and they certify their pets as therapy animals.

Small animals provide one form of lift; horses provide another. Equine-assisted therapy, which is actual therapy, helps people with physical and/or emotional needs. It is performed at ranches that have special programs. Most equine-assisted therapy centers welcome and even depend on volunteers. They perform the same kinds of tasks as volunteers on any ranch: barn work and leading or walking alongside riders. And they receive the same kind of satisfaction—the pleasure of having done hard work next to a wonderful animal—plus the knowledge that they are making a difference in someone's life.

Chapter Seven

VOLUNTEERING AT HOME

Zoos, shelters, and stables are great places where people who love animals can volunteer. But if the obvious places are not available, there are other options. People can work with animals in their own homes.

Foster Care

One type of in-home volunteering is foster care. Fostering an animal means assuming responsibility for total care of the animal until it is ready for a permanent home. Both shelters and animal rescue organizations frequently have animals they cannot care for in their facilities. Often these animals need more attention than typical pets. They may be babies that need to be fed during the night. They may be sick or recovering from a medical procedure and require careful monitoring. Sometimes rescued animals are wild or traumatized, and it takes a lot of tender love and care to settle them down and have them be comfortable with people. Rescue organizations and shelters cannot get these animals ready for adoption without volunteers who are willing to give them extra attention in their homes.

Who Is Helping Whom?

Alyssa's reason for volunteering was simple: she wanted to teach her ten-year-old son to give. She wasn't sure it would work, though, because she didn't know how the boy would do. Gabe had been through a lot, was seeing a counselor, and had nearly taken his own life. Alyssa chose an animal shelter for their volunteer experience and hoped Gabe could handle it.

Alyssa was surprised to discover that Gabe not only handled the responsibilities of the volunteer assignment, but also excelled at them. Animals that were afraid of adults took to the quiet boy. And what had begun as a one-time volunteer "lesson" turned into a several-times-a-week commitment. Gabe and his mother petted, played, and worked with animals that came to the shelter neglected or abandoned, making them ready to be adopted. People at the shelter started calling Gabe the "Dog Whisperer" because he could calm the frightened dogs and cats.

But the big benefit that Alyssa sees is not what Gabe is doing for the animals or for the shelter; what is more important is what volunteering with animals is doing for Gabe. As the dogs and cats trust him, he is learning to trust people. As he helps what he calls the "chicken dogs" come out of their shells, he is coming out of his. Volunteering has become a form of therapy for a hurting child; in giving, he is receiving.

Socializing Service Animals

Organizations that train service animals also depend on volunteers. Service animals are usually dogs that help people who have some type of special need. There are guide dogs for the blind, signal dogs for the hearing impaired, and dogs that are trained to respond to handlers who have frequent seizures. Mobility assistance dogs help people in wheelchairs, picking up items for them, turning light switches on and off, opening doors, etc. Dogs are trained specifically to serve handlers with medical challenges, psychiatric disorders, and autism.

Not all working dogs assist people with special needs. Some search, rescue, hunt, guard, herd, track, or detect various substances. This dog is training to work as a military dog.

Service dogs are intelligent, healthy, well-trained work animals. They are bred for their jobs, and their training starts when they are puppies. Long before formal instruction begins, they have to get used to being around people and other animals because that is what their work will require. They need to be comfortable in a variety of settings. Volunteers take the puppies into their homes and raise them as part of their families. They take them every-where they go, exposing them to all kinds of people, places, and situations. Service animals cannot be allowed to develop hab-its that would hinder their work. They have to be trained to obey commands without hesitation. Volunteers who take service dog puppies into their homes provide the experiences, discipline, and love that will be the foundation for their later instruction.

Providing Items

As much as zoos, shelters, and other animal organizations need volunteers, they also need many supplies. Volunteers can collect and deliver items that would make the animals more comfort-able and the jobs of the workers a little easier. Some recycled items that shelters can always use are:

- Newspapers for lining cages
- Shredded office paper for padding cages
- Plastic shopping bags for dog walkers
- Toilet paper and paper towel tubes for rabbits, guinea pigs, and hamsters to play with
- Old blankets for animal beds
- Old towels for bathing and cleaning up

This volunteer removes cats from their cage at an animal shelter so she can clean the enclosure. Many shelters depend on volunteers for this necessary job.

Volunteers who can sew might make padded beds for animal enclosures, curtains for their cages, or "Adopt Me" vests animals can wear when they are taken to pet stores or special events. Artistic volunteers can decorate Ping-Pong balls or plastic eggs as toys for cats. Cats also enjoy climbing structures and scratching posts, and volunteers can make these. Some shelters might accept homemade dog biscuits and treats.

Neighborhood Opportunities

Sometimes volunteer opportunities are as close as a friend or neighbor. People who work and people who are confined to their homes are often unable to give their pets the outside exercise they need. If they do not use a doggie daycare, they may be happy to have a trustworthy teen walk their dogs. Friends or neighbors who will be away from home for a day or longer often look for young people who will check in on their pets, feed them, and give them a little play time. They may need a pet sitter who will care for their animals in their homes while they are gone. These services can be offered on a volunteer basis, or they can be paid. Whether the work is volunteer or paid, in home or at another location, entry-level or requiring more experience, sharing one's time and talents to help an animal benefits the giver as much as the animal.

Chapter Eight

MAKING THE MOST OF THE OPPORTUNITY

Whether you are volunteering or interning for fun or for work experience, whether you want a career that involves animals or something else, your time volunteering can be of great benefit to you. Paying attention to some simple details during the experience and taking a few steps afterward will enable you to make the most of your volunteer opportunity.

While Volunteering or Interning

The importance of how you act during your volunteer or intern service is probably obvious, but it is crucial. You must display a good work ethic at all times—you never know what someone will notice. And you must treat everyone, even unreasonable people, politely—you never know who might play some role in your life in the future. Get to know as many people as you can. They can form a network of contacts that might introduce you to new opportunities.

Keep records of what you do. Write down the dates you volunteer and the names and contact information of the people you work with. These will come in handy when you look for employment and fill out a job application. When people compliment you, ask them to write notes and keep those notes in a file. They, too, will be useful in a future job search. List the responsibilities you have and the tasks you perform. If you can, take pictures and videos showing what you do. Consider having a blog, and make sure to update it regularly and keep it positive. Don't use it to complain; use it to demonstrate your knowledge and passion for what you are doing.

Interns from three different North Carolina universities return a loggerhead sea turtle to the ocean after treating it at a rescue and rehabilitation center.

Networking Pays Off

Jason Hofmann's parents always told him that if he did what he really loved, he would be successful. The trouble was that Jason didn't know what he really loved. He knew he liked animals, so he decided to start there. The first thing he did was work in a pet store.

The pet store was fun for a while, but he didn't really *love* it. He wanted to work directly with animals. Maybe being in a veterinary office would be more satisfying. So for five years, Jason served as a technician with a veterinarian. Some of the vet's clients noticed how good the young assistant was with their pets, and when they needed someone to sit with their dogs, they asked Jason.

Finally, Jason discovered what he really loved: taking care of dogs. He loved handling them, exercising them, grooming them, and nurturing them. He decided to open an in-home pet care business. He contacted the people whose dogs he had walked, and they referred their friends to him. The veterinarian for whom he had worked gave his name to his clients. The word spread quickly, and in three years Jason's business was making more than $100,000. As his parents predicted, he was successful because he did what he really loved...and he networked.

After Volunteering or Interning

As soon as your volunteer or intern experience ends, send a written thank-you letter. You may think you were the one who gave, but someone gave you the opportunity. Thanking people is always the right thing to do. In addition, the letter leaves your supervisor with a good impression of you.

Take some time to reflect on your experience. What did you learn about yourself? What did you learn about the field in which you volunteered? What skills did you acquire? What did you like and what did you dislike about the job? What do you wish you could have done? Write your reflections down so that you can refresh your memory later. Asking these questions will help you plan the next steps in your career journey. Do you want to volunteer again doing the same thing or something different? Do you want to try a completely new field? Do you want to take some classes or get some training? Are you ready to think about a job?

Preparing for the Future

No matter how far off those next steps may seem, don't miss the opportunity to include your volunteer and intern experiences in the preparation. Compile all of the information that you gathered—dates, names, achievements, notes and letters, pictures, awards, and reflections—and place it in a file. Much of the information can be used in writing a résumé. It can also be made into a portfolio. A résumé is a document describing you, your work history, and your qualifications for a particular job. A portfolio is a collection of materials that illustrates what you have done and what you can do.

This worker at San Diego Sea World is feeding Magellanic penguins. The flightless birds that live along the southern coasts of South America eat small fish, squid, krill, and other crustaceans.

Paper résumés and hard-copy portfolios have their uses, but many employers now expect electronic versions. You don't need to actually compose a résumé until you are ready to submit it because it needs to be tailored to the job for which you are applying. But you can start an e-portfolio, an electronic picture of your experiences and abilities. It enables you to store information online or on a removable disc, update it, manage it, and control who sees what parts of it. An e-portfolio is dynamic, which means it shows your growth over time. Programs are available for creating e-portfolios; school counselors can help you find one.

Electronic résumés and e-portfolios are part of your digital footprint. A digital footprint is an electronic trail you leave when you are online. It is made by all the places you have been that have your name on them: social media sites like Facebook and Twitter, video and picture-sharing sites such as YouTube and Flickr, and your own Web sites and blogs that you have created. Remember that nothing placed on the Internet ever really goes away. What you post will give anyone who wants to look a good picture of who you are and what you are like.

Today's employers follow your digital trail. If yours shows meaningful volunteer or intern experiences, they are sure to notice. A positive digital footprint that includes compassionate work with animals is a foot in the door to any job.

Glossary

apprentice A person who learns a trade or an art by working with another who is skilled in that area.

cattery A place that houses cats when their owners are away.

companion animal An animal that is a pet, as distinct from a service or work animal.

digital footprint The data trail, including personal information, created by a person's activities online.

docent An educator, usually a volunteer, who has been trained to give talks and answer questions about specific topics or fields.

equine Having to do with horses.

euthanize To put to death in a humane manner.

exotic Foreign; brought from another part of the world. An exotic animal is any species that is not native to the country.

habitat The area or environment in which a plant or animal normally and naturally lives.

intensive Concentrated on a single area or subject or into a short time; very thorough or demanding.

kennel An enclosed space for a dog or a facility that houses dogs while their owners are away.

marine Having to do with the ocean.

neuter To remove a male animal's testicles so that he cannot reproduce.

preserve An area of land that is protected and managed for the purpose of preserving, or keeping safe, particular animals and their habitats; a sanctuary.

purebred An animal of a certain breed whose ancestors for generations have been of the same breed with no other breed in the lineage.

sanctuary A protected area where homeless, abandoned, and abused animals live out their lives.

service animal An animal trained to provide some type of help to a person with a disability.

service learning A form of education at the elementary or high school level that combines classroom instruction with hands-on service activities in the community.

spay To remove the ovaries of a female animal so she cannot reproduce.

stipend An amount of money paid to someone for services performed or to offset that person's expenses. A stipend is generally lower than a salary for similar services.

tack The saddle, bridle, and other equipment horses wear so they can be ridden.

wrangler A person who handles horses.

For More Information

American Kennel Club (AKC)
8051 Arco Corporate Drive, Suite 100
Raleigh, NC 27617-3390
(919) 233-9767
Web site: http://www.akc.org
The AKC is an organization that promotes care and competition of purebred dogs. It provides resources for locating canine clubs, events, veterinarians, rescue groups, and other items of interest to dog owners.

American Sanctuary Association
2308 Chatfield Drive
Las Vegas, NV 89129
(702) 804-8562
Web site: http://www.asaanimalsanctuaries.org
This association is the accrediting organization that finds havens for homeless, abused, and abandoned animals. It provides a list of and links to accredited sanctuaries throughout the United States.

American Society for the Prevention of Cruelty to Animals (ASPCA)
424 East 92nd Street
New York, NY 10128
(212) 876-7700, ext. 4516
Web site: http://www.aspca.org

The ASPCA is an animal welfare organization that rescues
animals from abuse, works for legal protections for animals,
and provides resources to animal shelters and information
to the public.

Association of Zoos and Aquariums (AZA)
8403 Colesville Road, Suite 710
Silver Spring, MD 20910-3314
(301) 562-0777
Web site: http://www.aza.org
The AZA provides information and services to member zoos and
aquariums and information for the general public about animal care and wildlife conservation. Its Web site has links to
accredited zoos and aquariums and instructions for volunteering and applying for internships.

Canada's Guide to Dogs
Web site: http://www.canadasguidetodogs.com
This Web site enables users to find shelters, rescues, kennels,
dog clubs, daycares, groomers, and events for dogs near
them. It also contains information and articles on subjects of
interest to dog owners.

Canadian Association of Zoos and Aquariums (CAZA)
280 Metcalfe Street, Suite 400
Ottawa, ON K2P 1R7

Canada

(613) 567-0099 or (888) 822-2907

Web site: http://www.caza.ca

This is an association of the twenty-five leading zoological parks and aquariums in Canada. It promotes the welfare of zoo and aquarium wildlife and the advancement of science and conservation. Its Web site has links to accredited zoos and aquariums and instructions for volunteering and applying for internships.

Canadian Kennel Club (CKC)

200 Ronson Drive, Suite 400

Etobicoke, ON M9W 5Z9

Canada

(416) 675-5511

Web site: http://www.ckc.ca

Canada's national service organization promotes the advancement of purebred dogs. It recognizes, promotes, and publicizes actions of purebred dog owners.

Humane Society of the United States

2100 L Street NW

Washington, DC 20037

(202) 452-1100

Web site: http://www.humanesociety.org

An animal welfare organization, the Humane Society provides

ideas, programs, and resources for helping animals. Programs include rescue, adoption, sanctuaries, and rehabilitation.

National Audubon Society
700 Broadway
New York, NY 10003
(212) 979-3000
Web site: http://www.audubon.org
The National Audubon Society provides sanctuaries, programs, projects, and educational material dedicated to conserving and restoring natural ecosystems, focusing on birds and including other wildlife.

National Wildlife Federation (NWF)
11100 Wildlife Center Drive
Reston, VA 20190-5362
(800) 822-9919
Web site: http://www.nwf.org
The NWF protects and restores wildlife and its habitat and works with young people in various community volunteer programs to fit their interests.

Pet Sitters International
201 East King Street
King, NC 27021

(336) 983-9222

Web site: http://www.petsit.com

This is an educational association for professional pet sitters. It provides information and articles on pet care for a variety of animals, information and resources for beginning a pet sitting business, and a pet sitter locator.

U.S. Pony Clubs

4041 Iron Works Parkway

Lexington, KY 40511

(859) 254-7669

Web site: http://www.ponyclub.org

The club provides resources and materials for and about pony clubs. It has a locator for pony clubs nationally.

Web Sites

Due to the changing nature of Internet links, Rosen Publishing has developed an online list of Web sites related to the subject of this book. This site is updated regularly. Please use this link to access the list:

http://www.rosenlinks.com/FID/Anim

For Further Reading

Anderson, Laurie Halse. *Masks* (Vet Volunteers). London, England: Puffin, 2012.

Anderson, Laurie Halse. *Teacher's Pet* (Vet Volunteers). London, England: Puffin, 2009.

Bennett, Robin. *All About Dog Daycare...A Blueprint for Success*. Woodbridge, VA: Dream Dog Productions, 2005.

Berger, Sandra. *Ultimate Guide to Summer Opportunities for Teens: 200 Programs That Prepare You for College Success*. Waco, TX: Prufrock, 2008.

Boutelle, Veronica. *How to Run a Dog Business: Putting Your Career Where Your Heart Is*. Wenatchee, WA: Dogwise Publishing, 2011.

Boutelle, Veronica, and Rikke Jorgensen. *Minding Your Dog Business: A Practical Guide to Business Success for Dog Professionals*. Wenatchee, WA: Dogwise Publishing, 2010.

Byers, Ann. *Great Resume, Application, and Interview Skills*. New York, NY: Rosen Publishing, 2008.

Camenson, Blythe. *Opportunities in Zoo Careers*. Lincolnwood, IL: VGM Career Horizons, 1998.

Donovan, Sandra. *Volunteering Smarts: How to Find Opportunities, Create a Positive Experience, and More*. Minneapolis, MN: Twenty-First Century Books, 2012.

Gay, Kathlyn. *Volunteering: The Ultimate Teen Guide*. Lanham, MD: Scarecrow Press, 2007.

Green, Gail. *Animals and Teens: The Ultimate Teen Guide*. Lanham, MD: Scarecrow Press, 2009.

Hollow, Michele C., and William P. Rives. *The Everything Guide to Working with Animals*. Avon, MA: Adams Media, 2009.

Maynard, Thane. *Working with Wildlife: A Guide to Careers in the Animal World*. London, England: Franklin Watts, 2000.

Miller, Louise. *Careers for Animal Lovers and Other Zoological Types*. New York, NY: McGraw-Hill, 2007.

Niemeyer, Darlene. *Doggy Business 101: A Practical Guide to Starting and Running Your Own Business*. Neptune City, NJ: TFH Publications, 2009.

Palika, Liz, and Katherine A. Miller. *Animals at Work*. New York, NY: Howell Book House, 2009.

Reeves, Diane Lindsey, and Lindsey Clasen. *Career Ideas for Kids Who Like Animals and Nature*. New York, NY: Ferguson, 2007.

Shenk, Ellen. *Careers with Animals: Exploring Occupations Involving Dogs, Horses, Cats, Birds, Wildlife, and Exotics*. Mechanicsburg, PA: Stackpole, 2005.

Thornton, Kim Campbell. *Careers with Dogs: The Comprehensive Guide to Finding Your Dream Job*. Irvine, CA: Bow Tie Press, 2011.

Weinick, Suzanne. *Professional Connections: Learning How to Network*. New York, NY: Rosen Publishing, 2012.

Wilde, Nicole. *So You Want to Be a Dog Trainer*. 2nd ed. Santa Clarita, CA: Phantom, 2006.

Bibliography

ABC News Window on America. "Roseville Bear Relocation Project." 1995. Retrieved March 1, 2012 (http://www.youtube.com/watch?v=0MVmu4oJ99g&feature=related).

American Society for the Prevention of Cruelty to Animals. "Pet Statistics." Retrieved March 1, 2010 (http://www.aspca.org/about-us/faq/pet-statistics.aspx).

Association of Zoos and Aquariums. "Volunteer at an AZA-Accredited Zoo or Aquarium." Retrieved February 16, 2010 (http://www.aza.org/Education/KidsAndFamilies/detail.aspx?id=278).

DanWilton.com. "e-Portfolio Portal." Retrieved March 12, 2012 (http://www.danwilton.com/eportfolios).

Foltz-Gray, Dorothy. "The Healer." *Reader's Digest*, February 2012, p. 97.

Goodell, Mary Elizabeth. "Teen Volunteer Has Passion for Animals." *Augusta Chronicle*, September 6, 2010. Retrieved February 24, 2012 (http://chronicle.augusta.com/life/xtreme/2010-09-06/teen-volunteer-has-passion-animals).

NBC Real Life. "Person of the Week: Justin Barker." 1995. Retrieved March 1, 2012 (http://www.youtube.com/watch?v=fP8zXbcZrll&feature=related).

PawsitivelyTexas.com. "The Gift of Transformation—An Animal Shelter Volunteer's Story." January 8, 2012. Retrieved February 23, 2012 (http://pawsitivelytexas.com/a-bastrop-county-animal-shelter-volunteers-story).

Pet Sitters International. "Spotlight on Professional Pet Sitter, Jason Hofmann." Retrieved February 27, 2012 (http://www.petsit.com/ppsw-2011-jason-hofmann).

Presidential Pet Museum. "White House Pets." Retrieved February 27, 2012 (http://www.presidentialpetmuseum.com/whitehousepets-1.htm).

U.S. Pony Club. "The Pony Club Program." Retrieved March 3, 2010 (http://www.ponyclub.org/?page=PCProgram).

Voice. "Benji: The Frank Inn Story." April 1999. Retrieved March 2, 2012 (http://petticoat.topcities.com/benjifrankarticle.htm).

Zimmerman, Phyllis. "Susquehanna Township Teen Enjoys 'Amazing Opportunity' as Volunteer at Maryland Zoo in Baltimore." *Patriot News*, January 29, 2012. Retrieved March 1, 2012 (http://www.pennlive.com/midstate/index.ssf/2012/01/susquehanna_township_teen_enjo.html).

Index

About the Author

Ann Byers is a youth worker, writer, and editor who lives in Fresno, California. She has placed and supervised young people in a number of different volunteer positions. She is Zeke's grandmother (see Introduction).

Photo Credits